LIGHTNING BOLT BOOKS™

Dangerous Earthquakes

Carol Kim

Lerner Publications • Minneapolis

Lerner Publications Company
An imprint of Lerner Publishing Group, Inc.
241 First Avenue North
Minneapolis, MN 55401 USA

For reading levels and more information, look up this title at www.lernerbooks.com.

Main body text set in Billy Infant Regular. Typeface provided by SparkType.

Library of Congress Cataloging-in-Publication Data

Names: Kim, Carol, author.
Title: Dangerous earthquakes / Carol Kim.
Description: Minneapolis, MN: Lerner Publications, [2022] | Series: Lightning bolt books—earth in danger | Includes bibliographical references and index. | Audience: Ages 6-9 | Audience: Grades 2-3 | Summary: "Earthquakes happen when big plates of earth slide past one another. Powerful earthquakes can cause serious damage! Learn where earthquakes are common and how to stay safe, and hear from someone who survived an earthquake"—Provided by publisher.
Identifiers: LCCN 2021025142 (print) | LCCN 2021025143 (ebook) | ISBN 9781728441429 (library binding) | ISBN 9781728447933 (paperback) | ISBN 9781728444826 (ebook)
Subjects: LCSH: Earthquakes—Juvenile literature.
Classification: LCC QE534.3 .K56 2022 (print) | LCC QE534.3 ebook) | DDC 363.34/95—dc23

LC record available at https://lccn.loc.gov/2021025142
LC ebook record available at https://lccn.loc.gov/2021025143

Manufactured in the United States of America
1-49913-49756-8/13/2021

Table of Contents

The Ground Moves!

One moment all is calm. The next, the ground begins to shake. Hanging objects swing back and forth.

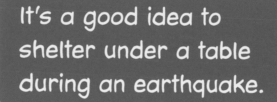

It's a good idea to shelter under a table during an earthquake.

Shelves and everything on them crash to the floor. It's an earthquake! A minute later, all is still. Then an aftershock hits.

When Earth's surface moves, it causes earthquakes. The outer layer of Earth is the crust. Earth's crust is made up of huge pieces called tectonic plates.

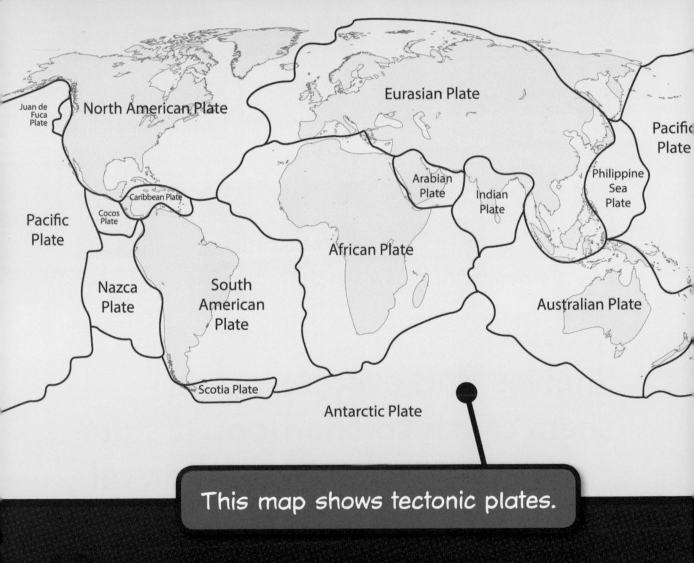

This map shows tectonic plates.

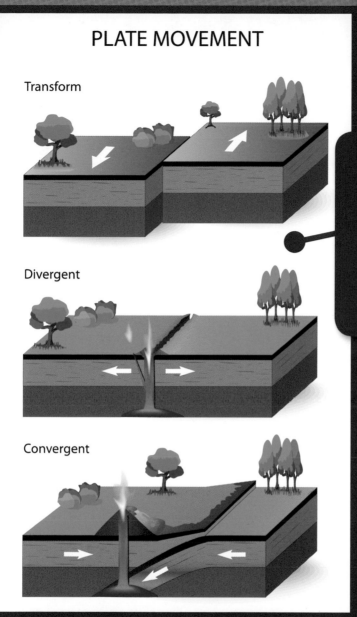

PLATE MOVEMENT

Transform

Divergent

Convergent

This image shows different ways tectonic plates can move.

These plates move all the time. When they move against one another, it causes the ground to shake.

Dangerous Earthquakes

Strong earthquakes can cause a lot of damage. Buildings can fall. Roads and bridges can break. Broken gas lines can cause fires.

Floods may damage homes and other buildings.

Earthquakes can damage levees and dams holding back water. If these break, the surrounding areas may flood. Earthquakes may shift loose earth or snow. Then landslides and avalanches can happen.

When a big earthquake strikes beneath the ocean, it can create a tsunami. This huge wave can wipe out everything in its path.

A tsunami destroyed parts of Indonesia in 2018.

These buildings in Nepal collapsed after an earthquake in 2015.

Earthquakes cause the most damage in areas where many people live. Falling buildings and flying objects hurt people.

Tracking Disaster

Scientists cannot predict earthquakes. But an early warning system exists. It can send an alert seconds before an earthquake hits.

EARTHQUAKE

The San Andreas Fault is a large fault line in California.

Earthquakes are most likely to occur along the edges of tectonic plates. These edges are fault lines.

This map shows the Ring of Fire. The red dots are large volcanoes.

Most major earthquakes happen in the Ring of Fire. This area circles the Pacific Ocean.

The strength of earthquakes is measured on the Richter scale. Minor earthquakes measure below 4.0. Earthquakes above 8.0 cause major destruction.

A seismograph shows how much the ground moves during an earthquake.

Earthquake Safety

If you are inside during an earthquake, get under a table or other furniture. If you are outside, move away from buildings and wires.

After a large earthquake, smaller quakes called aftershocks may soon follow.

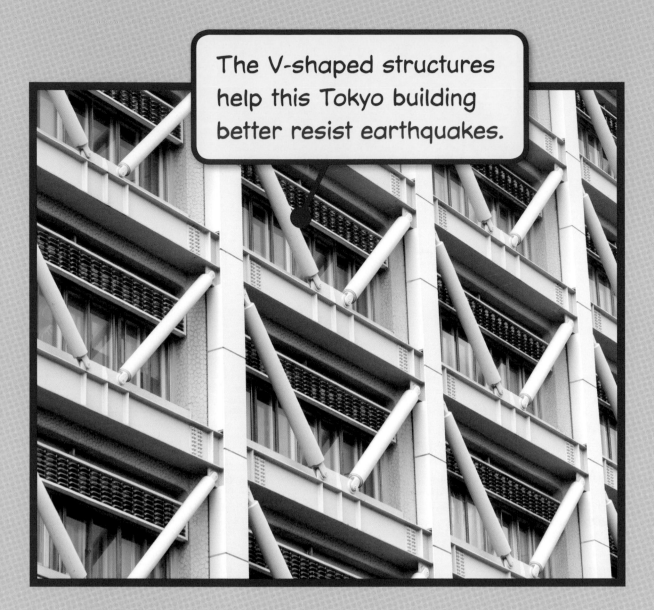

The V-shaped structures help this Tokyo building better resist earthquakes.

Many buildings are designed to survive earthquakes. Some slide back and forth on the ground. This helps them avoid damage.

Earthquakes are dangerous. But they helped form Earth's mountains and oceans. Earth would look very different without earthquakes!

The Appalachian Mountains were formed when tectonic plates crashed together.

I Survived an Earthquake

Sherra Cox had just switched on the 1989 World Series when the walls began to shake. Her home in Northern California fell around her. Cox was trapped. Firefighter Gerry Shannon had to crawl through the rubble, using a chain saw to cut a path to Cox. It took three hours to reach her. Cox told Shannon he was her hero after he pulled her free.

Earthquake Facts

- Millions of earthquakes happen every year. But most are so small or happen so far underground that people don't feel them.

- The 2004 Indian Ocean earthquake lasted nearly ten minutes. It was the longest-lasting earthquake ever recorded.

- Alaska has more earthquakes than any other state in the US.

- The strongest earthquake ever measured was 9.5 on the Richter scale. It happened in Chile in 1960.

Glossary

aftershock: an earthquake that happens soon after a stronger earthquake around the same location

avalanche: a large amount of snow or ice that suddenly slides down a mountain or hill

crust: the hard outer layer of Earth

dam: a barrier across a river or stream that holds back water

fault: a large break in Earth's crust between tectonic plates

landslide: a mass of earth and rocks that suddenly slides down a mountain or hill

levee: a structure built near a river to prevent flooding

Richter scale: a scale that measures the strength of an earthquake

tectonic plate: a large piece of Earth's crust that moves

tsunami: a very large, destructive wave caused by an underwater earthquake or volcano

Learn More

Kim, Carol. *Dangerous Floods*. Minneapolis: Lerner Publications, 2022.

Rathburn, Betsy. *Earthquakes.* Minneapolis: Bellwether, 2020.

Ready Kids: Earthquakes
https://www.ready.gov/kids/disaster-facts/earthquakes

Stark, Kristy. *Predicting Earthquakes*. Huntington Beach, CA: Teacher Created Materials, 2018.

US Geological Survey: Earthquakes for Kids
https://earthquake.usgs.gov/learn/kids/

Weather Wiz Kids: Earthquakes
https://www.weatherwizkids.com/weather-earthquake.htm

Index

Photo Acknowledgments

Image credits: jpgfactory/Getty Images, p. 4; maroke/Shutterstock.com, p. 5; Kolonko/ Shutterstock.com, p. 6; Designua/Shutterstock.com, p. 7; ollirg/Shutterstock.com, p. 8; Umam57/Shutterstock.com, p. 9; capture63/Shutterstock.com, p. 10; dutourdumonde/ Getty Images, p. 11; Becky Stares/Shutterstock.com, p. 12; Stocktrek/Getty Images, p. 13; Rainer Lesniewski/Getty Images, p. 14; Gary S Chapman/Getty Images, p. 15; Treetree2016/ Shutterstock.com, p. 16; Arctic-Images/Getty Images, p. 17; shigemi okano/Shutterstock. com, p. 18; Dave Allen Photography/Shutterstock.com, p. 19.

Cover: Dudarev Mikhail/Shutterstock.com.